FASCINATING STORIES FOR CURIOUS KIDS

Super Interesting Stories about History, Space, Animals, and Just About Anything Else You Can Think of

By

Dream Forge Publishing

Copyright © 2025 Dream Forge Publishing

All Rights Reserved.

Table of Contents

Introduction 1

Section 1: Fascinating Moments in History 5

    The Boy King's Tomb 7

    The Wright Brothers' and the First Flight 13

    The Great Fire of London 19

    The True Story of the Titanic 25

    The Secret Code of World War II 29

Section 2: The Wonders of Space and the Universe 33

    The First Moon Landing 35

    The Mystery of Black Holes 39

    The Mars Rover's Amazing Journey 43

    The Search for Alien Life 47

    The First Photo of a Black Hole 51

Section 3: Amazing Animals and Their Superpowers .. 57

    Hachiko The Loyal Dog 59

    The Elephant Who Cried 63

    Balto The Sled Dog Hero 67

    Ocean's Smartest Escape Artists 71

    The Journey of the Monarch Butterflies 75

Section 4: Unsolved Mysteries and Strange Phenomena 81

The Mystery of the Bermuda Triangle 83

The Dyatlov Pass Incident 87

The Vanishing Crew of the Mary Celeste 91

The Green Children of Woolpit 97

The Dancing Plague of 1518 101

Section 5: Great Inventors and Life-Changing Creations 105

Thomas Edison and the Light Bulb 107

The Accidental Invention of the Microwave 111

The Birth of the Internet 115

The Incredible Story of Braille 121

The First Artificial Heart 125

Section 6: Record-Breaking Feats and Extraordinary Human Achievements 129

The Tallest Building in the World 131

The First Journey to the Top 135

The Longest Time Living Underwater 139

Felix Baumgartner's Jump from Space 145

The Fastest Human on Earth 149

Conclusion 153

Introduction

Step into a world of astonishing real-life stories! This book is packed with incredible true tales that will take you on an unforgettable journey through history, science, space, nature, and groundbreaking human achievements. From mysteries waiting to be solved to record-breaking feats, each story will spark your curiosity and make you see the world in a whole new way. If you love exploring the unknown, uncovering fascinating discoveries, and learning about the wonders that shape our world, get ready—an exciting adventure awaits!

Have you ever wondered how a young boy became one of the most famous kings in history? Or how a small, simple invention changed the way we live forever? What about the secrets hidden deep in the ocean or the mysteries of space waiting to be explored? This book is packed with stories about real events, real people, and real discoveries that have shaped our world in the most fascinating ways.

Each chapter will introduce you to fearless explorers, brilliant inventors, record-breaking achievements, and even animals with unbelievable abilities! You'll travel back in time to uncover lost civilizations, witness groundbreaking scientific discoveries, and dive into the biggest mysteries of history and nature.

Imagine being there when the first airplane took flight, or witnessing the moment humans landed on the moon for the first time. Picture discovering an ancient Egyptian tomb hidden for thousands of years. These are the kinds of stories waiting for you in this book.

This book is all about adventure and wonder. Each story is written to make you think, imagine, and even feel like you are right there as history unfolds. You'll read about amazing human achievements, like how a blind boy invented a way for millions of people to read, or how a scientist accidentally discovered something in his pocket that changed how we cook forever.

You'll also discover some of the most astonishing animals on our planet—creatures that can communicate in ways we don't fully understand, survive in extreme conditions, or perform amazing feats that seem impossible. From the deep-sea creatures of the Mariana Trench to the fastest sprinter in history, this book is filled with mind-blowing true stories that will make you look at the world in a whole new way.

Some of these stories will inspire you, others will make you laugh, and a few might even leave you in shock. Did you know that some animals can predict earthquakes before they happen? Or that a man once jumped from the edge of space and lived to tell the tale? These are just a few of the incredible moments in history that you'll explore in this book.

No matter what kind of stories you love, there is something for everyone here. If you're curious, adventurous, and eager to learn about the world around you, then this book is the perfect companion.

So, are you ready to unlock the world's greatest true stories? Then turn the page and let the adventure begin!

Section 1: Fascinating Moments in History

The Boy King's Tomb

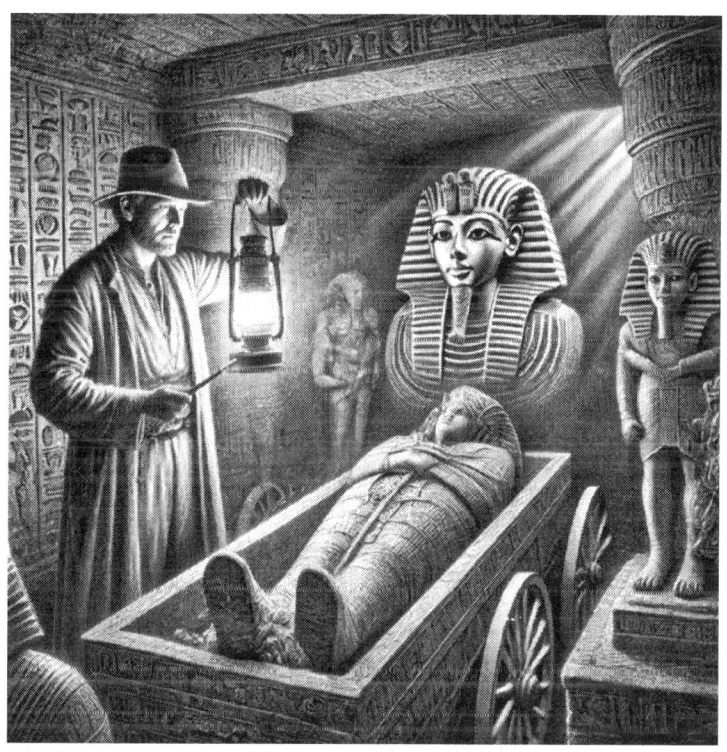

A long time ago, in the land of golden deserts and towering pyramids, a young boy became a king. His name was Tutankhamun, but most people today call him King Tut. He was just nine years old when he took the throne of ancient Egypt. Imagine that—while most kids were playing or learning to read, Tutankhamun was ruling an entire kingdom! But his reign didn't last long, and for thousands of years, his name was nearly forgotten. That is, until one of the greatest discoveries in history brought his story back to life.

In the early 1900s, many explorers searched for hidden tombs of Egyptian pharaohs. They believed that deep beneath the sand, untouched treasures were waiting to be found. One of these explorers was Howard Carter, a determined British archaeologist. He had spent years searching for King Tut's tomb, but most people believed it didn't exist. Many tombs in the Valley of the Kings had already been discovered, but Carter was certain there was one more secret buried beneath the sand.

His search had taken years, and his team was running out of money. His sponsor, Lord Carnarvon, was about to stop funding the expedition. But in November 1922, everything changed.

One morning, Carter's workers were digging in a new spot when they found something unusual—a step carved into the rock. As they dug deeper, more steps appeared, leading down into darkness. The team realized they had found the entrance to an undiscovered tomb!

Excited but cautious, Carter sent a message to Lord Carnarvon, who rushed to Egypt. When he arrived, they carefully broke through the door. Carter held up a candle and peered inside. As his eyes adjusted, he saw something that made his heart race—gold, everywhere!

When Lord Carnarvon asked if he could see anything, Carter replied with words that became famous: "Yes, wonderful things."

Inside the tomb, they found thousands of treasures. There were golden statues, jeweled necklaces, weapons, chariots, and even board games that belonged to the young pharaoh. Everything was perfectly preserved, as if waiting for King Tut to return. But the greatest discovery was yet to come.

As Carter's team carefully cleared the treasures, they found another sealed door. Beyond it was the burial chamber. And inside that chamber lay the most extraordinary find of all—King Tut's sarcophagus.

The sarcophagus was a large, golden coffin. Inside, there were three more coffins, each inside the other. The final one, made of solid gold, held the mummy of King Tut himself. His face was covered by a beautiful golden mask, decorated with blue lapis lazuli and precious stones.

It was the first time in history that a nearly intact royal tomb had been found. Other tombs had been robbed by thieves long ago, but King Tut's treasures were untouched for over 3,000 years.

Although his tomb was filled with treasures, King Tut's life was still a mystery. Scientists later studied his mummy and found that he died at just 19 years old. But how?

Some believed he was murdered, but modern research suggests he may have died from illness or an injury. His tomb also seemed unfinished, leading some to believe he died unexpectedly, and his burial was rushed.

Not long after the tomb was opened, strange things started happening. Lord Carnarvon, who funded the discovery, died suddenly from an infected mosquito bite. Soon after, several others connected to the expedition also became sick or died under mysterious circumstances.

People began to whisper about "The Curse of the Pharaohs," a legend that warned anyone who disturbed an ancient tomb would face bad luck. But scientists believe there's no real curse—just coincidences and possibly ancient bacteria inside the tomb.

Even though King Tut only ruled for a short time, he became the most famous pharaoh in history because of the discovery of his tomb. Today, his golden mask and treasures are displayed in museums, and people from all over the world travel to Egypt to see where he was buried.

Thanks to Howard Carter's discovery, the boy king will never be forgotten. His story, filled with mystery, treasure, and adventure, continues to fascinate people of all ages—including you!

The Wright Brothers' and the First Flight

On a cold, windy morning in December 1903, two brothers stood on the sandy dunes of Kitty Hawk, North Carolina, preparing to do something that had never been done before. Orville and Wilbur Wright, bicycle mechanics from Ohio, had spent years working on an invention that people had dreamed about for centuries—a machine that could fly. Many thought they were crazy. After all, humans weren't meant to fly. But the Wright brothers believed otherwise.

Ever since they were kids, Orville and Wilbur had been fascinated by how birds soared through the sky. They spent hours watching them, noticing how they tilted their wings to stay balanced. Their father once brought home a small flying toy, a helicopter-like contraption made of rubber bands and wood. The boys were amazed as it lifted into the air. From that moment on, they were determined to build something even bigger—something that could carry a person.

The road to their first flight wasn't easy. There were no instructions, no textbooks, and no experts to guide them. Every attempt at building a flying machine ended in failure, broken parts, and bruised egos. Other inventors had tried, and most had given up after their designs crashed. But the Wright brothers were different. Every time something went wrong, they studied their mistakes, made adjustments, and tried again.

By 1902, after countless experiments, they had built a glider that could stay in the air. But gliding wasn't enough—they wanted powered flight. They needed an engine, but no one made one small and light enough for their aircraft. So, they built their own. They also designed propellers using their knowledge of bicycles, believing that air worked in a similar way to the resistance they had studied on bike tires.

With their plane, called the Wright Flyer, finally ready, the brothers took it to Kitty Hawk. This place was chosen because of its strong winds and soft sand, perfect for testing their invention. Wilbur won the coin toss to be the first pilot, but his first attempt ended in a minor crash. The damage was repaired, and three days later, it was Orville's turn.

It was December 17, 1903. Orville climbed onto the wooden aircraft, lying flat on his stomach, gripping the controls. Wilbur steadied the wings as the engine roared to life. The propellers spun, kicking up sand. And then, with a sudden push forward, the machine lifted off the ground.

For 12 seconds, the world changed forever.

It wasn't a long flight—only 120 feet, shorter than the length of a basketball court. But it was enough. The Wright Flyer had done the impossible—it had flown. The brothers took turns piloting the machine that day, each flight going a little farther, a little longer. Wilbur's final flight of the day lasted 59 seconds, covering 852 feet.

The news of their success spread slowly. At first, many people refused to believe it. Some thought their claims were exaggerated, while others ignored them entirely. But the Wright brothers didn't care. They had proven that flight was possible, and they were just getting started.

They continued refining their designs, making each new plane stronger, faster, and easier to control. By 1905, they had a plane that could stay in the air for over 30 minutes. Still, few people outside their small group of supporters took them seriously. It wasn't until 1908, when Wilbur demonstrated their aircraft in France, that the world finally took notice. Crowds gathered to watch in awe as he soared above them, turning and circling effortlessly.

Suddenly, everyone wanted to fly. Governments, businesses, and adventurers all saw the potential of airplanes. Within a few years, planes were being used for transportation, military operations, and mail delivery. The Wright brothers had not only invented the airplane but had opened the door to the future of aviation.

Orville and Wilbur didn't seek fame or fortune. They simply wanted to prove that human flight was possible. They worked side by side for years, always pushing the boundaries of what was possible. Wilbur passed away in

1912, but Orville lived long enough to see airplanes evolve into powerful machines that could cross oceans and even break the sound barrier.

What began as two boys watching birds turned into one of the greatest achievements in history. Today, every time a plane takes off, it carries with it the spirit of those 12 seconds at Kitty Hawk—a moment that changed the world forever.

The Great Fire of London

The summer of 1666 was hot, dry, and restless in the city of London. For months, the sun had baked the wooden houses and narrow streets, turning them into a tinderbox just waiting for a spark. The people of London went about their daily lives, unaware that one night would change their city forever.

It all began in a small bakery on Pudding Lane. The bakery belonged to Thomas Farriner, a baker who supplied bread to the King's navy. On the night of September 2, 1666, as the city slept, a tiny flame flickered inside his oven. Thomas and his family went to bed without realizing that a stray ember had landed on some dry flour sacks nearby. Within moments, the fire began to grow. The flames crept along the wooden walls, hungry and unstoppable. By the time Thomas woke up, his bakery was engulfed in a raging fire.

Shouting for help, Thomas and his family scrambled to escape. They climbed out of a window onto the roof, but their maid was too scared to follow. The fire swallowed the bakery, and she became the first victim of what would become one of the most devastating disasters in London's history.

The flames spread quickly, leaping from house to house. In 1666, London was a city of narrow streets and wooden buildings, packed tightly together. Most people used open flames for cooking and lighting, and there was no organized fire brigade like we have today. Buckets of water were not enough to stop the fire, and before dawn, the wind had carried the flames far beyond Pudding Lane.

As the sun rose, panic gripped the city. The fire roared like a monster, eating everything in its path. People ran through the streets carrying whatever they could—children, pets, bags of coins, and even their mattresses. Some threw their belongings into the River Thames, hoping to save them from the flames. Others fled in boats, watching in horror as the city behind them turned into a sea of fire.

By midday, the fire had reached St. Paul's Cathedral, one of the most important buildings in London. The great church, which had stood for centuries, was thought to be safe because of its stone walls. But inside, wooden scaffolding fed the flames, and soon the mighty cathedral collapsed in a fiery explosion. Molten lead from its roof flowed down the streets like lava.

King Charles II knew that something had to be done. He ordered men to pull down houses in the fire's path, hoping that creating gaps would stop the flames from spreading. But the fire was moving too fast. For four days, the inferno raged, reducing 13,000 homes, 87 churches, and countless businesses to ashes.

On September 6, the winds finally died down, and the fire burned itself out. The city lay in ruins—charred, broken, and smoking. Thousands of people were left homeless, sleeping in the fields outside London. Miraculously, only a few people died, but the destruction was enormous. The heart of London had been wiped away.

In the aftermath, accusations flew. Some blamed foreign spies, others suspected criminals. A man named Robert Hubert, a foreign watchmaker, falsely confessed to starting the fire and was executed, even though historians later proved he wasn't even in London when the fire began. The truth was, the fire had simply been an accident, fueled by dry weather, wooden buildings, and strong winds.

But from disaster came rebirth. Instead of rebuilding the city exactly as it was, King Charles II and architect Sir Christopher Wren planned a better, stronger London. New buildings were made of brick and stone instead of wood, making them safer from future fires. A modern fire service was developed, and strict building codes were introduced to prevent another catastrophe.

One of the greatest changes came with the rebuilding of St. Paul's Cathedral. Christopher Wren designed a new cathedral that still stands today, its massive dome a symbol of London's strength and survival.

The Great Fire of London was a disaster, but it also became a turning point. It forced the city to rethink safety, rebuild stronger, and emerge from the ashes with a new spirit. Today, if you walk through London, you'll find a small plaque on Pudding Lane marking where the fire began, and the great dome of St. Paul's standing tall—a reminder that even after the worst disasters, new beginnings are always possible.

The True Story of the Titanic

On a cold, clear night in April 1912, the Titanic, the grandest ship ever built, sailed across the Atlantic Ocean on its first voyage. It was a floating palace, designed to be unsinkable, with luxurious cabins, grand staircases, and even a swimming pool. The ship carried 2,224 passengers and crew, from the wealthiest people in the world to immigrants seeking a new life in America. Everyone believed the Titanic was the safest ship ever made. But within a few short days, that belief would be shattered forever.

The Titanic set sail from Southampton, England, on April 10, 1912, heading for New York City. Passengers marveled at its size and elegance. Wealthy travelers enjoyed lavish meals, music, and grand ballrooms, while those in third class had smaller rooms but still found comfort compared to the ships they had traveled on before.

For four days, the journey was smooth. But beneath the calm waters, danger lurked. Icebergs were common in the North Atlantic, and despite warnings from other ships, Titanic's crew believed the ship could handle anything. The captain, Edward Smith, even allowed the ship to continue at full speed, confident that nothing could harm it.

Then, at 11:40 PM on April 14, 1912, a lookout spotted something massive ahead—a dark, looming iceberg. He rang the alarm, and the crew tried to steer the ship away. But it was too late. The iceberg scraped along the side of the Titanic, tearing a 300-foot gash in its hull. At first, many passengers didn't realize anything had happened. There was no loud crash, no sudden jolt. But deep below, water rushed into the lower decks, flooding the compartments meant to keep the ship afloat.

At first, many believed the Titanic was safe. After all, it had been built with 16 watertight compartments, designed to prevent sinking. But the iceberg had damaged too many of them. Slowly, the front of the ship began to dip into the ocean.

As the truth became clear, panic set in. There weren't enough lifeboats—Titanic had only 20, enough for about half the people on board. Crew members began rushing passengers to the boats, women and children first. Some lifeboats left half-full, while many people, especially third-class passengers, struggled to reach the upper decks.

The ship's band played music, trying to calm the frightened crowd. But the situation grew worse by the minute. Titanic's stern lifted high into the air, and the great ship snapped in half. Within moments, the Titanic disappeared beneath the icy waves, leaving hundreds of people struggling in the freezing water.

More than 1,500 lives were lost that night. Some froze within minutes, while others clung to debris, hoping for rescue. Only one lifeboat returned to look for survivors. The lucky 710 people who made it into lifeboats were eventually picked up by a passing ship, the Carpathia, in the early hours of April 15.

News of the disaster shocked the world. How could the unsinkable ship sink on its first journey? An investigation revealed several reasons: the ship was moving too fast, there weren't enough lifeboats, and many warnings about icebergs had been ignored. The tragedy led to major changes in ship safety, including requiring lifeboats for all passengers and better communication at sea.

Today, the Titanic lies 12,500 feet below the ocean, its wreck discovered in 1985. Scientists and explorers have visited the site, uncovering furniture, dishes, and even shoes left behind. But beyond the artifacts, the story of Titanic remains a lesson in human ambition, bravery, and loss.

More than a century later, the Titanic is not just a shipwreck—it is a story of dreams, tragedy, and survival that continues to captivate the world.

The Secret Code of World War II

29

During World War II, the world was at war, and every country was searching for a way to outsmart its enemies. The United States needed a way to send secret messages without the enemy figuring them out. If enemy forces intercepted military orders, they could change the course of the war. Codes had been used before, but enemies always managed to break them. The U.S. needed a code that was unbreakable—and they found their answer in an unexpected place.

Far from the battlefields, deep in the deserts and mountains of the American Southwest, lived the Navajo people. The Navajo were Native Americans with a unique language that very few people outside their community understood. Their language was complex, had no written form, and was nearly impossible for outsiders to learn.

A man named Philip Johnston, who had grown up on a Navajo reservation, realized that the Navajo language could be the perfect solution. He proposed using Navajo soldiers to create a secret military code. The U.S. Marine Corps agreed to give it a try, and in 1942, they recruited 29 Navajo men to create the first-ever Navajo Code.

These brave young men, later known as the Navajo Code Talkers, were sent to a military base, where they created a special code using their language. Instead of using simple words, they assigned Navajo words to different military terms. For example, they used the word "turtle" for a tank, "chicken hawk" for a dive bomber, and "whale" for a battleship. Letters of the alphabet were also represented by Navajo words.

But this was not just speaking Navajo—this was a carefully crafted code within their own language, making it impossible for enemy forces to understand. The first test was a success. The code was fast, accurate, and completely unbreakable.

As the U.S. fought against Japan in the Pacific, the Navajo Code Talkers were sent to the front lines. They were in the middle of the action, sending and receiving secret messages in the heat of battle. Instead of using radios or written messages, they would speak the coded messages aloud to each other using field telephones. Within seconds, orders were sent across battlefields, helping American troops prepare for attacks, call for reinforcements, and even trick the enemy.

One of the biggest tests of the Navajo Code came during the Battle of Iwo Jima in 1945, one of the most important battles of the war. For three days straight, six Navajo Code Talkers transmitted over 800 messages without a single mistake. Thanks to their efforts, U.S. troops were able to capture the island, a major victory in the Pacific War.

The Japanese army, which had been skilled at breaking American codes before, was completely confused. No matter how hard they tried, they could never crack the Navajo Code. It remained the only unbroken military code in history.

The Navajo Code Talkers played a huge role in helping the U.S. win the war. Their bravery and quick thinking saved countless lives. But despite their efforts, they did not receive public recognition for many years. Their work was so secret that it remained classified until 1968, long after the war ended.

When their story was finally made public, the Navajo Code Talkers were hailed as heroes. In 2001, the original 29 Code Talkers were awarded the Congressional Gold Medal, one of the highest honors in the United States.

Today, their legacy lives on. The Navajo Code Talkers proved that sometimes, the most powerful weapon isn't a gun or a tank, but intelligence, skill, and language. Their incredible story remains a symbol of bravery, innovation, and cultural strength—and their code will always be remembered as the one code that could never be broken.

Section 2: The Wonders of Space and the Universe

The First Moon Landing

On July 20, 1969, the world held its breath as three astronauts traveled farther than anyone had ever gone before. Neil Armstrong, Buzz Aldrin, and Michael Collins were on a mission to do something no human had ever done—land on the moon.

Their spacecraft, Apollo 11, had launched from Cape Kennedy, Florida, on July 16, 1969. It was a giant rocket, taller than a 30-story building, with enough power to escape Earth's gravity and travel 240,000 miles to the moon. The journey took four days, and the astronauts had to live in a tiny space capsule, eating dried food, floating in zero gravity, and checking their equipment every hour.

When Apollo 11 finally reached the moon's orbit, the astronauts prepared for the most daring part of their mission. Armstrong and Aldrin climbed into a small spacecraft called the Eagle, leaving Collins behind in the main command module to orbit the moon. The Eagle began its descent, but something was wrong—a warning light started flashing. Mission Control back on Earth debated whether to abort the landing, but Armstrong, calm and focused, took manual control of the spacecraft. He realized they were heading toward a dangerous, rocky area and needed to find a safe place to land.

With only 30 seconds of fuel left, Armstrong finally found a flat spot and guided the Eagle down. Then, at 4:17

PM, his voice came through the radio: "Houston, Tranquility Base here. The Eagle has landed."

The world erupted in cheers and celebration. Millions of people had been watching on their televisions, and now it was official—humans had landed on the moon!

A few hours later, at 10:56 PM, Neil Armstrong opened the hatch and climbed down the ladder. As he stepped onto the moon's surface, he said the words that would become famous forever:

"That's one small step for man, one giant leap for mankind."

For the first time in history, a human was walking on another world. The moon's surface was covered in fine gray dust, and Armstrong's boots left the first-ever footprints on the moon. Buzz Aldrin joined him shortly after, describing the moon as a "magnificent desolation." The two astronauts hopped and bounced, discovering that the moon's gravity was much weaker than Earth's, making them feel lighter.

They planted an American flag, took photographs, and collected moon rocks and dust samples to bring back to Earth. They also placed a plaque that read:

"Here men from the planet Earth first set foot upon the Moon, July 1969 A.D. We came in peace for all mankind."

After spending 21 hours on the moon, Armstrong and Aldrin climbed back into the Eagle and blasted off to rejoin Collins in the command module. They left behind some equipment, an American flag, and even their footprints, which will remain untouched for millions of years since there's no wind on the moon.

On July 24, 1969, Apollo 11 splashed down in the Pacific Ocean, where the astronauts were picked up by a Navy ship. They had done it—they had made history.

The moon landing was more than just an achievement for the United States. It was a moment that united the world, proving that with hard work, courage, and determination, nothing is impossible. Even today, people look up at the moon and remember the bravery of the Apollo 11 crew—the first humans to take a giant leap for mankind.

The Mystery of Black Holes

For centuries, people have looked up at the night sky, wondering about the secrets of the universe. Among the most mysterious objects in space are black holes—invisible monsters that can swallow entire stars and bend time itself. They are some of the strangest and most powerful things in existence, but for a long time, scientists didn't even know if they were real.

The idea of black holes started with Albert Einstein's theory of relativity in 1915. He discovered that space and time could be warped by massive objects like planets and stars. Some scientists wondered: What would happen if a star collapsed into something so small and dense that nothing—not even light—could escape? That's how the idea of black holes was born.

But for decades, black holes remained just that—an idea. No one had ever seen one because black holes don't give off light. They were completely invisible, hidden deep in space. It wasn't until the 1960s that astronomers found evidence that black holes were real. They discovered Cygnus X-1, a massive, unseen object pulling in gas from a nearby star. The way the gas spiraled around it at incredible speeds suggested that something powerful and invisible was lurking there—a black hole.

Black holes form when huge stars run out of fuel and collapse under their own gravity. When this happens, the star's core shrinks into an incredibly tiny space, but its gravity becomes so strong that nothing can escape it—not even light. The boundary around a black hole is called the event horizon. Anything that crosses this point—whether it's a planet, a spaceship, or even time itself—can never return.

Black holes come in different sizes. Some are just a few times the size of our Sun, while others are millions or even billions of times bigger. These are called supermassive black holes, and scientists believe that one lies at the center of almost every galaxy, including our own Milky Way.

One of the biggest questions about black holes is: What happens inside them? Since nothing can escape, it's impossible to know for sure. Scientists believe that time slows down near a black hole, and if you fell into one, you would be stretched into a long, thin shape—something they call spaghettification! It sounds like science fiction, but it's based on real physics.

For years, black holes remained a mystery. Then, in 2019, something incredible happened—scientists captured the first-ever photograph of a black hole. Using a network of telescopes around the world, they took an image of the supermassive black hole in the center of a galaxy called M87. The picture showed a glowing ring of hot gas surrounding a dark, shadowy center—the event horizon. It was the first time humanity had ever seen a black hole with their own eyes.

But the mystery of black holes doesn't stop there. Some scientists believe they might hold the key to understanding the universe itself. Could they lead to other dimensions? Do they act as gateways to different parts of space and time? No one knows for sure. Even Stephen Hawking, one of the greatest scientists of all time, spent his life trying to figure out the secrets of black holes.

One thing is certain—black holes are among the most fascinating and powerful objects in the universe. They remind us that space is full of mysteries, waiting to be explored. Every time we look up at the stars, we are one step closer to unlocking the secrets of these cosmic giants. The more we learn, the more we realize how much is still unknown.

And who knows? Maybe one day, we'll send a spaceship to the edge of a black hole, ready to explore one of the greatest mysteries of the universe.

The Mars Rover's Amazing Journey

For centuries, humans have looked up at the night sky and wondered if life exists beyond Earth. One planet has always been of particular interest—Mars, the Red Planet. It's cold, dusty, and covered in giant mountains and deep canyons. But could it have once had water, life, or even secrets we haven't yet discovered? To find out, scientists sent rovers—robotic explorers designed to brave the harsh Martian landscape and uncover its mysteries.

The journey to Mars is no easy task. It's millions of miles away, and it takes months for a spacecraft to travel there. But despite the challenges, NASA and other space agencies have sent multiple rovers to explore Mars. These robotic scientists have helped us learn more about the planet than ever before.

One of the first successful rovers was Spirit, which landed on Mars in 2004 along with its twin, Opportunity. Their mission? To search for signs of past water, test the soil, and take pictures of the Martian surface. Spirit faced harsh conditions, getting stuck in soft sand and battling extreme cold, but it sent back incredible images of rocky hills and dusty plains. Opportunity, on the other hand, was a record-breaker—it was only supposed to last 90 days but ended up working for 15 years, traveling over 28 miles across the planet!

Then came Curiosity, one of the most famous rovers ever. It landed on Mars in 2012 using a daring sky-crane system that gently lowered it onto the surface. Curiosity was built to search for ancient life—not little green aliens, but clues that Mars might have once been able to support bacteria and other tiny organisms. One of its biggest discoveries was evidence of ancient riverbeds, proving that water once flowed on Mars.

But perhaps the most exciting rover yet is Perseverance, which landed on February 18, 2021. Its mission is even more ambitious: searching for signs of ancient life and collecting samples that could one day be brought back to Earth. Unlike previous rovers, Perseverance carried something truly special—Ingenuity, the first-ever flying helicopter on another planet. Ingenuity made history by taking controlled flights in Mars' thin atmosphere, proving that powered flight is possible on another world!

Perseverance has also been exploring Jezero Crater, an ancient lakebed that scientists believe might have once supported life. Using high-tech instruments, it is analyzing Martian rocks, searching for signs of microbial fossils, and helping scientists understand whether humans could one day live on Mars.

But why are we sending rovers to Mars in the first place? Scientists believe that understanding Mars' past can help us prepare for the future. If humans ever travel to Mars, we need to know what challenges we'll face, where to find water, and how to survive in an environment so different from Earth.

Mars rovers have already taught us so much, but the adventure isn't over yet. The next big step? A manned mission to Mars! NASA and other space agencies are working on plans to send humans to the Red Planet in the coming decades. If all goes well, astronauts could walk on Mars within our lifetime.

The journey of the Mars rovers is a testament to human curiosity, innovation, and the desire to explore the unknown. They have shown us a world once thought impossible to reach, proving that with determination and science, nothing is out of our grasp. Who knows? Maybe one day, the first astronaut to step on Mars will have been inspired by the discoveries of these incredible robotic explorers. Until then, the rovers continue their mission, uncovering the secrets of the Red Planet, one wheel rotation at a time.

The Search for Alien Life

For as long as humans have gazed at the night sky, we've asked one big question: Are we alone in the universe? Scientists have spent decades searching for signs of alien life, looking for clues on distant planets, deep in space, and even in our own solar system. Could there be tiny life forms hiding beneath the surface of Mars? Could strange creatures live in the frozen oceans of distant moons? Or are there advanced civilizations out there, waiting to be discovered?

The search for alien life starts with one key ingredient—water. Every living thing on Earth needs water to survive, so scientists believe that finding water on other planets or moons is the best way to find life beyond Earth.

Mars has long been one of the most exciting places to search for life. NASA's Curiosity and Perseverance rovers have found ancient riverbeds, dried-up lakes, and evidence that liquid water once flowed across the planet's surface. While no living creatures have been found, scientists believe that Mars might have supported tiny life forms billions of years ago. If life once existed there, could it still be hiding underground?

But Mars isn't the only place scientists are looking. Some of the best chances of finding alien life may actually be on moons rather than planets. One of the most promising places is Europa, a moon of Jupiter. Even though it's covered in thick ice, scientists believe there's a vast ocean beneath its frozen surface. Since life on Earth began in the ocean, could something similar be happening on Europa?

Another exciting target is Enceladus, one of Saturn's moons. This icy world has huge geysers that shoot water into space. When NASA's Cassini spacecraft flew through one of these geysers, it detected organic molecules—building blocks of life. Could tiny creatures be swimming in Enceladus's underground ocean?

Beyond our solar system, scientists are searching for Earth-like planets orbiting other stars. These are called exoplanets, and thanks to powerful telescopes like the Kepler Space Telescope and the James Webb Space Telescope, thousands have been discovered. Some of these exoplanets are in the habitable zone, meaning they might have the right conditions for liquid water—and possibly life.

But what if alien life isn't just tiny bacteria or simple creatures? What if intelligent beings are out there? Scientists have been listening for radio signals from space, hoping to pick up messages from advanced civilizations. This is called the Search for Extraterrestrial Intelligence (SETI). So far, no confirmed signals have been found, but in 1977, a mysterious radio signal called the "Wow! Signal" was detected. It lasted only 72 seconds and never repeated, but to this day, no one knows where it came from. Could it have been a message from an alien world?

Scientists have even sent our own messages into space, hoping that if intelligent aliens are out there, they might find them. In 1974, the Arecibo Telescope sent a coded radio message toward a distant star system. The Voyager 1 and Voyager 2 probes, launched in 1977, carry Golden Records—discs containing sounds of Earth, music, greetings in different languages, and even recordings of whale songs. If an alien civilization ever finds them, they'll have a glimpse of life on Earth.

The search for alien life is one of the most exciting mysteries in science. Every year, we discover new exoplanets, learn more about the strange moons in our solar system, and develop better technology to search the stars. Maybe in the future, a rover will find microbial fossils on Mars, a spacecraft will detect life in Europa's ocean, or a radio telescope will finally hear a message from another civilization.

Until then, the question remains: Are we alone in the universe? Or is someone—or something—out there waiting to be discovered? The search continues, and one day, we may finally have the answer.

The First Photo of a Black Hole

For centuries, black holes were one of the greatest mysteries of space. Scientists knew they existed, but no one had ever seen one. Since black holes swallow even light, they were completely invisible. The only way scientists could prove they were real was by studying how they pulled on nearby stars and galaxies. But in 2019, something incredible happened—for the first time in history, humans captured an actual photograph of a black hole.

The journey to this discovery started many years before. Scientists had spent decades trying to understand black holes. Albert Einstein's Theory of Relativity, published in 1915, predicted their existence. Later, famous physicist Stephen Hawking studied them and made groundbreaking discoveries about how black holes behave. Even though scientists had proof that black holes existed, no telescope on Earth was strong enough to actually see one—until the Event Horizon Telescope (EHT) project changed everything.

The Event Horizon Telescope wasn't just one telescope—it was a network of eight telescopes from around the world, working together to create a giant, planet-sized camera. This was necessary because black holes are incredibly far away, and capturing an image of one would require more power than any single telescope could provide. By linking observatories across the globe, scientists created a telescope powerful enough to look deep into space and find something that had never been seen before.

The target of their search was a supermassive black hole located in the center of the galaxy Messier 87 (M87), which is about 55 million light-years away from Earth. This black hole is 6.5 billion times the mass of our Sun—one of the largest black holes ever discovered. Scientists spent years gathering data, but there was still one major problem—how do you take a picture of something that doesn't emit light?

The answer was to capture the shadow of the black hole. Even though black holes themselves are invisible, they have an edge called the event horizon—a point where nothing, not even light, can escape. Around this edge, swirling hot gas and dust create a glowing ring, which can be seen from Earth using powerful telescopes. Scientists believed that if they could detect this glowing ring, they could finally "see" a black hole.

In April 2017, the telescopes of the Event Horizon Telescope began their work. Over several nights, they collected massive amounts of data—so much that it couldn't be sent over the internet. Instead, the data was stored on hard drives and flown to a supercomputer for processing. Scientists spent two years piecing together the image, using advanced computer algorithms to turn radio signals into a visual photograph.

Then, on April 10, 2019, the world finally saw it—the first-ever image of a black hole. The picture showed a dark circle surrounded by a bright, glowing orange ring. This wasn't just a blurry photo; it was proof that black holes exist exactly as scientists predicted. The dark circle was the black hole's shadow, and the glowing ring was the hot gas being pulled toward it.

The image shocked the world. People everywhere were amazed by the idea that we could actually see something so far away, so mysterious, and so powerful. Scientists were especially excited because the image perfectly matched Einstein's predictions, proving that his Theory of Relativity was correct once again.

This discovery was only the beginning. The success of the Event Horizon Telescope inspired scientists to take even better images of black holes. In 2022, they captured the first image of the black hole at the center of our own galaxy, the Milky Way—a supermassive black hole called Sagittarius A*. With more advanced technology, future telescopes might even be able to create video footage of black holes in action, helping us learn even more about these cosmic giants.

The first photo of a black hole is one of the greatest achievements in space exploration. It proves that with science, teamwork, and determination, we can uncover even the most hidden secrets of the universe. There are still many mysteries left to solve—what happens inside a black hole? Do they lead to other dimensions? Could they be connected to the birth of new galaxies? These are questions that scientists continue to explore.

One thing is certain—black holes are no longer just ideas in physics books. They are real, and we have seen them with our own eyes. The universe is full of wonders, and as we keep looking, who knows what incredible discoveries will come next?

Section 3: Amazing Animals and Their Superpowers

Hachiko The Loyal Dog

In the bustling city of Tokyo, Japan, during the 1920s, a small Akita dog named Hachiko was born. No one could have guessed that this puppy would one day become one of the most famous and beloved dogs in the world, a symbol of loyalty and devotion that would inspire generations.

Hachiko's story began in 1924, when a kind-hearted professor named Hidesaburo Ueno adopted him. Professor Ueno was a university professor who lived near Shibuya Station, one of the busiest train stations in Tokyo. From the moment Hachiko became part of his family, the two were inseparable.

Every morning, Professor Ueno would leave for work, and Hachiko would walk with him to Shibuya Station. As the professor boarded his train, Hachiko would sit patiently and watch him leave. Then, like clockwork, every evening, Hachiko would return to the station to wait for his owner, happily greeting him when he stepped off the train.

Day after day, this routine continued. The people at the station—commuters, workers, and shopkeepers—noticed the faithful dog waiting for his owner. Many smiled at the sight, thinking Hachiko was just another happy pet welcoming his beloved human.

But then, something tragic happened. On May 21, 1925, Professor Ueno suffered a sudden stroke while at work. He never came home.

Hachiko didn't understand what had happened. That evening, as always, he went to Shibuya Station, patiently waiting for his owner to return. But Professor Ueno never stepped off the train.

Still, Hachiko refused to give up. Every single day, he returned to the station, sitting in his usual spot, watching every train that arrived, hoping to see his owner walk through the doors. Days turned into weeks, and weeks turned into months, but Hachiko never stopped waiting.

At first, the station workers and passengers were confused—why was this dog still coming to the station every evening? Some people tried to shoo him away, thinking he was a stray. But others who knew the story of Professor Ueno realized what was happening. Hachiko was waiting for someone who would never return.

Soon, the entire community grew to love and admire Hachiko. The station workers fed him, and kind strangers brought him food and water. Rain, snow, or sunshine, Hachiko never missed a day. He waited at the station for nearly 10 years, proving a level of loyalty that touched the hearts of everyone who saw him.

In 1932, a newspaper reporter learned about Hachiko's incredible devotion and wrote an article about him. The story spread all across Japan, and suddenly, Hachiko became a national symbol of loyalty. People traveled from all over just to see the faithful dog at Shibuya Station.

As the years passed, Hachiko became older and weaker, but he still continued his daily journey to the station. Finally, on March 8, 1935, Hachiko passed away near the place where he had waited for nearly a decade.

The people of Japan mourned his loss, and to honor his devotion, a bronze statue of Hachiko was built at Shibuya Station. Even today, the statue stands in the same place where he once waited, reminding the world of his unbreakable bond with his owner.

Hachiko's story continues to inspire people everywhere. His tale has been told in books, movies, and even school lessons, teaching the importance of love, loyalty, and never giving up on the ones we care about.

Today, if you visit Shibuya Station, you'll see hundreds of people gathering around Hachiko's statue, taking pictures and remembering the story of a dog whose loyalty lasted a lifetime. Hachiko may have been just one dog, but his devotion made him unforgettable.

The Elephant Who Cried

In the vast jungles of India, where towering trees sway in the wind and rivers cut through the dense forests, lived an elephant named Raju. For fifty long years, Raju had known nothing but pain, chains, and captivity. He was not born into freedom, but instead, he was taken from his mother as a baby and sold into a life of misery.

From a young age, Raju was forced to work for different owners, each treating him with cruelty and neglect. He was used for begging, beaten with sticks, and chained so tightly that the heavy metal dug into his skin. His legs were bound with spiked shackles that caused painful wounds. He was never fed properly, surviving only on scraps of food that passersby would throw at him. Some days, he ate paper or plastic, just to fill his empty stomach.

For half a century, Raju had never known kindness. He had never felt the warmth of love or the joy of roaming free. Every day was the same—painful, exhausting, and lonely. But deep inside, Raju never lost hope.

Then, one fateful day in 2014, everything changed. A team of rescuers from an animal welfare group called Wildlife SOS heard about Raju's suffering. They knew they had to save him, but it wouldn't be easy. His owner had kept him chained for so long that he refused to let him go, seeing the elephant as nothing more than a source of money.

But the rescuers refused to give up. They worked with forest officials and police officers, and after careful planning, they launched a midnight rescue mission. Under the cover of darkness, they approached Raju, who stood silent and weary, his eyes reflecting decades of pain.

As the rescuers cut away his chains, something extraordinary happened—tears began rolling down Raju's face. He was crying, just like a human would. The rescuers were overwhelmed with emotion. It was as if Raju knew he was finally free, that after fifty years of suffering, someone had come to save him.

It took hours to remove the heavy chains that had weighed him down for so long. When the last shackle fell, Raju took his first steps of freedom. His legs were weak, his body frail, but his spirit was unbroken. The rescuers led him into a truck, taking him to an elephant sanctuary, where he would never be hurt again.

For the first time in his life, Raju walked on soft grass instead of hot pavement. He bathed in cool waters, splashing and playing like a young elephant. He ate fresh fruits, filling his stomach without fear of hunger. But most importantly, he felt kindness for the first time.

Other rescued elephants at the sanctuary greeted him, wrapping their trunks around him in a gentle embrace. It was their way of saying, "Welcome home."

Day by day, Raju's wounds healed, not just on his body, but also in his heart. He no longer flinched when humans approached him. He learned to trust again. He made friends with other elephants, playing, roaming, and enjoying the life he had always deserved.

Raju's story spread around the world. People were amazed that an elephant had cried real tears and that, despite everything, he had never lost hope. His rescue inspired many to fight for animal rights, ensuring that no elephant would ever suffer the way he had.

Today, Raju lives happily in the sanctuary, surrounded by nature and friends. He is no longer a prisoner of chains but a symbol of resilience, survival, and the power of kindness. His story reminds us that even in the darkest times, there is always hope—and sometimes, the smallest act of kindness can change a life forever.

Balto The Sled Dog Hero

The frozen wilderness of Alaska is one of the toughest places on Earth. In the winter, temperatures drop so low that even breathing feels like ice. Snow and blizzards make travel nearly impossible, and the people who live there depend on sled dogs to carry supplies across the frozen land. But in 1925, something terrible happened in the small town of Nome, Alaska—a deadly disease began to spread, and the only hope for survival rested on the shoulders of a brave sled dog named Balto.

It all started when children in Nome began to fall seriously ill. Doctors quickly realized that they were suffering from diphtheria, a dangerous disease that could close a child's throat and make it impossible to breathe. The only way to save them was with a special medicine called antitoxin, but there was one big problem—the nearest supply was over 600 miles away, in a city called Anchorage.

In 1925, there were no airplanes that could fly in blizzards, and the train could only take the medicine part of the way. The last 674 miles would have to be traveled by dog sled teams, racing against time through ice, snow, and deadly storms. It was a dangerous journey, but without the medicine, many people—especially children—would not survive.

A relay of 20 mushers (sled drivers) and their sled dog teams were chosen for the mission, called the Serum Run. Each team would take the medicine part of the way, handing it off like a baton in a race. One of the most experienced mushers, Leonhard Seppala, had the fastest team, led by his champion dog, Togo. Togo and his team raced an incredible 260 miles, battling fierce winds and temperatures as low as -60°F.

When the serum was passed to Gunnar Kaasen, he had one last leg of the journey—53 miles through one of the worst storms Alaska had ever seen. Leading his team was Balto, a strong and determined sled dog who had never been a lead dog before. Many believed he was not fast enough, but Kaasen trusted Balto to guide them through the storm.

The blizzard was so strong that Kaasen could barely see his own hands, let alone the trail. If they took one wrong turn, they could be lost forever in the snow. But Balto kept running, his keen sense of smell guiding the team through blinding winds.

At one point, strong winds knocked Kaasen and the sled over, sending the serum flying into the snow. With his hands frozen, Kaasen struggled to find it, but Balto stood strong, waiting for him to recover. He knew they could not fail.

Balto and his team raced through the darkness, pushing forward with every ounce of strength. After what seemed like an eternity, the lights of Nome appeared in the distance. Exhausted but determined, Balto pulled the sled into town, delivering the life-saving medicine just in time.

Not a single vial of the medicine was lost, and thanks to the heroic efforts of the sled dog teams, the children of Nome were saved.

Balto became a legend overnight. Newspapers across the country celebrated him as a hero. In the same year, a statue of Balto was placed in Central Park, New York City, with the words:

"Endurance, Fidelity, Intelligence."

Balto and the other sled dogs proved that courage and determination can overcome even the harshest obstacles. His incredible journey remains one of the greatest animal hero stories of all time, a reminder that even in the coldest and darkest times, a brave heart can lead the way.

Ocean's Smartest Escape Artists

The ocean is home to some of the most mysterious and intelligent creatures on Earth, but few are as fascinating as the octopus. With their eight arms, soft bodies, and ability to change color in an instant, octopuses are true masters of disguise. But what really sets them apart is their incredible intelligence. They can solve puzzles, escape from tanks, use tools, and even outsmart predators in ways that seem almost magical.

Unlike fish, octopuses have no bones, which allows them to squeeze into the tiniest cracks and crevices. This ability makes them expert escape artists. There have been countless stories of octopuses sneaking out of aquariums, slipping through tiny openings, and even breaking into other tanks to steal food!

One of the most famous octopus escape stories happened in New Zealand in 2016. An octopus named Inky lived in the National Aquarium, where he was well cared for and loved by visitors. But one night, Inky decided he wanted to explore the outside world. When a small gap was accidentally left in the top of his tank, he made his move. He climbed out of the tank, slid across the floor, and found a drainpipe that led directly to the ocean. By the time the staff arrived in the morning, Inky was gone—back to the wild, where he belonged.

Octopuses aren't just great at escaping; they are also problem solvers. Scientists have given them mazes, locked boxes, and puzzles, and time after time, they have figured out how to unlock doors and find hidden food. Some have even been seen using coconut shells as shields, carrying them around and hiding inside when they feel threatened—like a real-life superhero with a secret hideout!

Another amazing skill octopuses have is their ability to blend into their surroundings. Using special skin cells called chromatophores, they can change color and texture in the blink of an eye, making them invisible to predators. One moment, an octopus looks like a rock; the next, it vanishes into the coral reef.

Some octopuses take their disguise even further. The mimic octopus can pretend to be other sea creatures! It can change its shape to look like a sea snake, a lionfish, or even a jellyfish, scaring away predators who might want to eat it.

But perhaps the most incredible thing about octopuses is their brainpower. Unlike humans, who have most of their neurons in their brains, octopuses have neurons spread throughout their arms. This means that each arm can think and move on its own, even if it's separated from the body! Some scientists believe that octopuses might be as smart as dogs or even small children.

In fact, octopuses are so smart that some scientists believe they might even dream. Researchers have observed octopuses changing colors while they sleep, suggesting that they might be experiencing dreams just like humans do. What could an octopus be dreaming about? Maybe a daring escape or a delicious meal waiting to be found!

Despite their incredible abilities, octopuses have short lifespans. Most live only a few years, and some species survive for just six months. But in that short time, they manage to outsmart predators, solve puzzles, escape from danger, and explore the ocean like true adventurers.

Today, octopuses continue to amaze scientists, divers, and ocean lovers everywhere. They remind us that intelligence comes in many forms, and sometimes, the most brilliant minds aren't on land, but hidden deep beneath the sea. Whether they're sneaking out of tanks, solving puzzles, or disappearing before our eyes, one thing is clear—octopuses are the ocean's greatest escape artists!

The Journey of the Monarch Butterflies

Every year, something incredible happens in the world of butterflies. Millions of monarch butterflies, delicate and brightly colored, take off on an epic journey across North America. These tiny creatures, weighing less than a paperclip, travel thousands of miles—farther than any other butterfly species in the world. This journey is one of nature's most mysterious and breathtaking events, and scientists are still trying to understand how these fragile insects accomplish such an incredible feat.

The story begins in Canada and the northern United States, where monarch butterflies hatch and grow during the warm summer months. As the days become colder and food becomes scarce, the butterflies know it's time to leave. But instead of staying in one place, they begin an extraordinary migration southward, heading toward the warm mountains of Mexico and California.

Unlike birds or whales, monarch butterflies have never taken this journey before. The ones that leave in the fall are not the same butterflies that made the trip the previous year. Yet, somehow, they know exactly where to go. Scientists believe this ability is built into their DNA—something like a natural compass inside their tiny bodies that guides them toward the right destination.

The migration is dangerous. The butterflies must fly over mountains, forests, rivers, and even the vast Gulf of

Mexico. Along the way, they face strong winds, sudden storms, and predators like birds and spiders. To survive, they glide on air currents to save energy, stopping at fields and gardens to drink nectar from flowers.

After traveling for up to 3,000 miles, the monarchs finally reach their winter homes—the forests of central Mexico and coastal California. These special forests provide the exact conditions they need to survive the winter: cool temperatures, high humidity, and protection from harsh weather. Here, millions of butterflies gather, clustering together in huge groups on tree branches, covering the trees in orange and black. This creates one of the most spectacular sights in nature—entire forests filled with butterflies, their wings fluttering like falling leaves in the wind.

The monarchs rest here for several months, waiting for spring. When the temperature rises, they begin their journey back north, but here's the amazing part—they don't complete the return trip alone. Instead, the monarchs lay eggs along the way, and their children continue the journey. It takes four or five generations of butterflies to make it all the way back to Canada and the United States, completing the full migration cycle.

Each generation plays a role in this great journey of monarchs plays a role in this great journey. The butterflies that hatch in spring and summer live only a few weeks, quickly laying eggs and continuing the journey northward. But the ones born in late summer—the ones that begin the migration south—are special. They are called the "super generation." These butterflies live up to nine months, much longer than their parents or grandparents, so they can complete the long migration to Mexico.

Despite their incredible journey, monarch butterflies face serious threats today. Their numbers have dropped in recent years because of deforestation, climate change, and the loss of wildflowers that provide nectar for their long flight. The destruction of milkweed plants—the only plant monarch caterpillars eat—has also made it harder for them to survive.

Scientists and conservationists are working to protect the monarchs by planting more milkweed, preserving forests, and raising awareness about their migration. Schools, gardeners, and wildlife groups across North America have joined the effort to create butterfly-friendly spaces, ensuring that future generations of monarchs can continue their journey.

The monarch butterfly's migration is one of the greatest natural wonders of the world. It reminds us that even the smallest creatures are capable of extraordinary feats. Their journey is a story of strength, survival, and determination, proving that even the most delicate wings can carry a spirit strong enough to cross continents.

So, the next time you see a monarch butterfly fluttering past, remember—you might be witnessing a traveler on one of the most remarkable migrations in nature!

Section 4: Unsolved Mysteries and Strange Phenomena

The Mystery of the Bermuda Triangle

For years, sailors and pilots have told eerie stories about a strange and mysterious place in the Atlantic Ocean—a place where ships and planes vanish without a trace. This place is known as the Bermuda Triangle, and it has puzzled scientists, explorers, and conspiracy theorists for decades. Some believe it is a supernatural force, while others think it's just bad weather and human error. But one thing is certain—the Bermuda Triangle remains one of the greatest mysteries of the modern world.

The Bermuda Triangle is a large stretch of ocean between Miami, Florida; Bermuda; and Puerto Rico. It covers over 500,000 square miles of open water. For centuries, people have sailed through this area without trouble. However, strange things have also happened—ships have disappeared without sending distress signals, planes have gone missing from radar screens, and entire crews have vanished, leaving behind empty vessels drifting at sea.

One of the most famous disappearances happened in 1918 when the USS Cyclops, a massive Navy cargo ship, vanished without a trace. The ship had 306 crew members on board, and despite extensive searches, no wreckage was ever found. There were no distress calls, no clues, nothing—it was as if the ship had just vanished into thin air.

Another well-known case is that of Flight 19, a squadron of five U.S. Navy bombers that took off from Florida in 1945 for a routine training mission. The weather was clear, and the pilots were experienced, but as they flew over the Bermuda Triangle, something strange happened. Their radio transmissions became confusing and disoriented. The lead pilot reported that their compasses weren't working and that they couldn't tell which direction was west. Then, one by one, the planes disappeared from radar. A rescue plane was sent to find them, but it vanished too. To this day, none of the planes or crew members have ever been found.

Over the years, more and more strange disappearances have been reported in the Bermuda Triangle. Some people believe that there is something supernatural at work—perhaps aliens, time warps, or even underwater cities like Atlantis pulling ships and planes into another dimension. Others think that the magnetic fields in the area could be interfering with navigational instruments, causing pilots and sailors to become lost.

Scientists, however, have a more logical explanation. They believe that the Bermuda Triangle is a very dangerous part of the ocean—not because of magic, but because of natural forces. The area is known for sudden and powerful storms, massive ocean currents, and deep underwater trenches where wreckage could quickly sink out of sight. The Gulf Stream, a strong ocean current that flows through the Triangle, can carry debris over vast distances, making it almost impossible to find wreckage.

Another theory is that methane gas from the ocean floor could be responsible for the disappearances. Scientists have discovered large pockets of methane trapped under the seabed. If this gas suddenly erupts, it could create huge bubbles that make the water lose its ability to support ships, causing them to sink almost instantly. The gas could also rise into the air, affecting airplane engines and causing them to fail. Despite all the stories, most scientists agree that the Bermuda Triangle is not as mysterious as people think. While disappearances have happened, they are not more common there than in any other heavily traveled area of the ocean. In fact, thousands of planes and ships travel through the Bermuda Triangle every year without any problems.

So, is the Bermuda Triangle really a portal to another world, or is it just a part of the ocean where bad weather and human mistakes happen? The truth may never be fully known. But one thing is certain—the mystery of the Bermuda Triangle will continue to capture imaginations for generations to come. Whether it's fact or fiction, the legend of the Bermuda Triangle remains one of the greatest unsolved mysteries of the sea.

The Dyatlov Pass Incident

The Dyatlov Pass Incident is one of the most mysterious and chilling stories in history. It's a true tale that has puzzled scientists, adventurers, and detectives for more than 60 years. A group of nine experienced hikers set out on a journey through the snowy mountains of Russia, but none of them returned. When rescuers finally found them, their campsite was in ruins, and what they discovered was so strange and unexplained that it has remained an unsolved mystery to this day.

It all began in January 1959, when a group of nine hikers, led by a young man named Igor Dyatlov, set out on an expedition to the Ural Mountains in Soviet Russia. They were all experienced adventurers, used to tough conditions, and their goal was to reach the top of a mountain called Kholat Syakhl, which means "Dead Mountain" in the local Mansi language.

The group traveled by train, bus, and skis, documenting their trip with photographs and diary entries. Everything seemed normal. They laughed, made jokes, and took pictures in the snow. Their last recorded entry showed them setting up camp on a mountainside, preparing for the night. But after that, no one ever heard from them again.

When they didn't return as expected, rescue teams set out to find them. What they discovered was terrifying and completely unexplainable.

The rescuers found the hikers' tent abandoned and ripped open from the inside. It looked as if they had cut their way out in a panic and fled into the freezing night without their shoes, jackets, or any warm clothing. Their footprints in the snow led down the mountain for a while—then suddenly disappeared.

As the search continued, rescuers began to find the bodies—some near a forest, some buried under snow, and some in strange, unnatural positions. The first two were found near a burnt-out fire, dressed in only their underwear, as if they had been trying to stay warm. Others were discovered further away, frozen solid. But the most bizarre part came when they found the last four hikers.

Their bodies had severe and unexplained injuries—one had a crushed skull, two had broken ribs, and one was missing her tongue. Yet, there were no signs of struggle or an avalanche that could have caused these injuries. Even stranger, some of their clothes had traces of radiation! Scientists, investigators, and conspiracy theorists have spent decades trying to understand what happened that night. Some believe the hikers panicked because of an avalanche, but their tent wasn't buried, and the injuries didn't match avalanche patterns. Others think they were attacked by something or someone, but there were no signs of a fight or footprints from another person.

One theory suggests strong winds created a sound that caused extreme panic, making the hikers flee their tent in terror. Others believe they accidentally wandered into a military test zone, where secret weapons or radiation might have caused their injuries.

But perhaps the strangest theory of all? Some believe a yeti, or a wild creature, might have attacked them. While there is no solid proof, the hikers' behavior that night was so unusual that many believe something scared them beyond reason. To this day, the Dyatlov Pass Incident remains one of the world's greatest unsolved mysteries. In 2019, Russian authorities reopened the case and ruled that an unusual type of avalanche might have been responsible, but many still don't believe it. The mystery lives on, and the snow-covered mountains of Dyatlov Pass remain a place of eerie silence—a reminder of a journey that ended in a way no one can explain.

Whether it was nature, a tragic accident, or something far more mysterious, the story of Dyatlov Pass continues to fascinate people around the world. Even today, adventurers visit the site, searching for clues to unlock the secrets hidden in the snow. But the truth? It may never be known.

The Vanishing Crew of the Mary Celeste

The Mary Celeste is one of the most famous ghost ships in history. It was a strong, well-built sailing vessel, yet something terrifying happened that turned it into one of the greatest mysteries of the sea. In 1872, the ship was found drifting in the Atlantic Ocean, completely abandoned. There was no sign of the captain, crew, or passengers—it was as if they had vanished into thin air. To this day, no one knows what really happened, and the mystery of the Mary Celeste remains one of the strangest unsolved sea stories of all time.

The journey of the Mary Celeste began on November 7, 1872, when it left New York Harbor, sailing toward Genoa, Italy. On board were Captain Benjamin Briggs, his wife Sarah, their two-year-old daughter Sophia, and a crew of seven experienced sailors. The ship carried barrels of alcohol, which were being transported to Europe. Everything seemed normal as the ship set sail, moving steadily across the Atlantic.

But then, something inexplicable happened. On December 5, 1872, nearly a month later, another ship, the Dei Gratia, was sailing through the same waters when its crew spotted a vessel drifting strangely in the distance. It was the Mary Celeste. At first, they thought it was just another ship making its way through the ocean, but as they got closer, they realized something was very wrong.

The Mary Celeste was sailing without anyone at the helm—there was no captain, no crew, no passengers. The ship was completely silent. Concerned, the sailors from the Dei Gratia boarded the ship, expecting to find an explanation. Instead, what they found was deeply disturbing.

Everything on board looked perfectly normal—almost as if the crew had just stepped away for a moment. The cargo was untouched, and there were no signs of a struggle. The crew's belongings, including clothing and personal items, were still there. Even the captain's logbook, which recorded daily events, was in place, with its last entry written on November 25, days before the ship was found.

The only thing missing? The people.

There was no sign of where they had gone or why they had abandoned the ship. Even stranger, the ship's only lifeboat was gone, but there were no distress signals, no damage, and no signs of bad weather. The Mary Celeste was simply floating, empty, and abandoned in the middle of the ocean.

The mystery shocked the world. What could have possibly made a trained crew, a captain, and his family leave a perfectly good ship behind? Over the years, many theories have tried to explain what happened, but none have been proven.

Some believe the crew may have panicked over the alcohol cargo, fearing that leaking fumes could cause an explosion. If they abandoned ship, thinking it was about to blow up, they might have gotten lost at sea, unable to find their way back.

Others think they might have been attacked by pirates, but no valuables or cargo were stolen. Some theories suggest a giant sea creature, like a massive squid, dragged them into the depths—but that seems more like a tale from a pirate's legend than real history.

One of the most chilling theories suggests that the crew was overtaken by madness, possibly due to food poisoning or contaminated drinking water, leading them to jump overboard in confusion. Another idea is that they were caught in a sudden waterspout or freak wave, which could have caused them to abandon ship in a panic, only for the ship to survive the storm without them.

Despite countless investigations, the truth has never been discovered. The Mary Celeste was eventually brought back to shore, but the fate of its crew remains a mystery. It has become one of the most haunting legends of the sea, a real-life ghost ship that continues to puzzle historians, sailors, and mystery lovers alike.

Even today, as ships cross the Atlantic, some sailors whisper about the vanishing crew of the Mary Celeste, wondering what really happened on that fateful journey. Perhaps the sea will never give up its secrets.

The Green Children of Woolpit

The Green Children of Woolpit is one of the strangest and most mysterious stories in history. It happened hundreds of years ago, in a quiet village in England, but to this day, no one can explain where these children came from, why their skin was green, or what truly happened to them. Some believe they were lost travelers from another land, while others think they may have come from a hidden world beneath the Earth. It is a story that has puzzled historians and storytellers for generations.

The tale begins in the 12th century, in the small village of Woolpit, England. Back then, England was a place of knights, castles, and mystery. Woolpit was a simple farming village, surrounded by thick forests and deep pits, which had been dug long ago to trap wolves.

One day, as the villagers were tending to their fields, they made a shocking discovery—two strange children, a boy and a girl, appeared out of nowhere near one of the wolf pits. They looked like normal children in many ways, but there was one bizarre difference—their skin was green.

The villagers rushed to them, speaking to them in English, but the children seemed terrified and confused. They didn't understand the language and were dressed in strange clothes made from an unfamiliar material. The boy and girl clung to each other, clearly frightened, and they refused to eat any of the food the villagers offered them.

For days, the children ate nothing, until they were finally given raw beans, which they devoured hungrily. It was the only food they would eat. As time passed, they slowly learned to eat other things, and their green skin faded to a more normal color.

The villagers took them in and cared for them, but still, no one knew where they had come from. When they finally learned to speak English, they told an unbelievable story.

The children claimed they had come from a land of eternal twilight, where the sun never shined. In their world, everything had a greenish glow, including the people who lived there. They said they had been herding their father's cattle when they heard a loud bell ringing. As they followed the sound, they suddenly found themselves in the bright world of Woolpit, where the sun was far brighter than anything they had ever seen.

No one knew what to make of their story. How could such a place exist? Was it deep underground, in a hidden valley, or another dimension entirely? Some believed they had wandered from a distant land, while others whispered that they had come from a magical world beneath the Earth, perhaps from the legendary Hollow Earth or a secret fairy kingdom.

Sadly, the boy did not survive for long. He became weak and sickly soon after arriving in Woolpit and eventually passed away. The girl, however, grew up among the villagers and was baptized. She later worked in a nobleman's household and lived a relatively normal life, though she was always considered different.

Over the centuries, many have tried to explain the mystery of the Green Children. Some believe they were lost orphans from a nearby village, suffering from a disease that made their skin appear green. Others think they escaped from an underground cave system, where they had been trapped away from sunlight for so long that their skin changed color. And then, there are those who believe something far stranger—that the children were from another world, either a hidden kingdom beneath the Earth or even another planet. Could they have traveled through a secret passage, a portal, or a rift in time?

We may never know the truth, but the story of the Green Children of Woolpit remains one of the most mysterious and fascinating tales of all time. Even today, people still wonder: Who were they? Where did they come from? And could there be other hidden worlds waiting to be discovered? The mystery remains unsolved, leaving behind only questions, wonder, and the eerie memory of two children with green skin who stepped into history—and then, almost as suddenly, disappeared.

The Dancing Plague of 1518

In the summer of 1518, in the town of Strasbourg, France, something very strange happened. A woman named Frau Troffea stepped into the street and began to dance. There was no music, no celebration—just her, twirling, stomping, and spinning, as if she couldn't stop. People gathered around, confused by what they were seeing. But the strangest part? She kept dancing for hours, then days, without rest.

At first, the townspeople thought she was simply enjoying herself or maybe acting strangely. But after a few days, others began to join her. First, it was a few people, then dozens, and within a week, more than 400 people were dancing non-stop. They danced in the streets, in the markets, and in front of houses. They danced day and night, unable to stop—even when their feet were bruised and bleeding.

No one knew why this was happening. The dancers were not celebrating; they were in pain, and many begged for help. But they couldn't stop. Some collapsed from exhaustion, while others suffered from heart attacks or strokes. A few even danced to their deaths.

The local authorities panicked. The town's leaders thought the dancers might be suffering from hot blood, an ancient belief that the body could overheat and cause madness. Their solution? More dancing! They built a wooden stage, hired musicians, and hoped that by letting the people dance it out, the strange spell would end on its own. But instead, the opposite happened—the music made even more people join in.

Weeks passed, and the people of Strasbourg were desperate for answers. Priests believed the dancers were possessed by spirits or cursed by Saint Vitus, a saint associated with dancing. Some thought it was punishment from God, while others believed it was caused by witchcraft or demonic forces.

As the weeks dragged on, the city finally realized that forcing people to dance wasn't helping. The authorities changed their approach. Instead of music, they sent the dancers to a mountain shrine to pray for forgiveness and healing. Slowly, the strange plague began to fade. One by one, the dancers stopped. The spell had finally been broken.

But even centuries later, no one knows exactly what caused the Dancing Plague of 1518. Historians and scientists have come up with different theories.

One theory is that the people were suffering from mass hysteria, a rare psychological phenomenon where large groups of people fall into a shared panic or trance. This could have been triggered by extreme stress, fear, and hardship—things that were common in 1518.

Strasbourg had been suffering from disease, famine, and poverty, which might have pushed people into a state of mental and emotional distress.

Another theory is that the dancers may have accidentally eaten a toxic mold called ergot, which grows on damp rye bread. This mold can cause hallucinations, muscle spasms, and strange behavior. It's the same substance that later led to the discovery of LSD, a powerful hallucinogenic drug. If the people of Strasbourg had unknowingly consumed this mold, it could explain why they felt compelled to dance without stopping.

Some even wonder if it was a religious or spiritual experience—a kind of trance or ritual that got out of control. There are records of other dancing plagues happening in Europe during the Middle Ages, though none were as large or deadly as the one in Strasbourg.

Whatever the reason, the Dancing Plague of 1518 remains one of the strangest medical mysteries in history. How did it start? Why did so many people join in? And what made it finally stop? Even today, scientists and historians still don't have all the answers.

One thing is certain: for weeks in the summer of 1518, an entire town was caught in a mysterious and terrifying dance, and to this day, no one knows exactly why.

Section 5:
Great Inventors and Life-Changing Creations

Thomas Edison and the Light Bulb

In the late 1800s, the world was a very dark place once the sun went down. People relied on candles, oil lamps, and gas lights to see at night, but these methods were dangerous, expensive, and didn't last long. Cities were dim, homes were filled with smoke from burning oil, and factories had to stop work when it got too dark. But one man would change everything—a man named Thomas Edison.

Thomas Edison was one of the greatest inventors in history. He was born in 1847 in the United States and was always curious about how things worked. As a child, he loved science experiments and was known for asking endless questions. Though he struggled in school, his love for learning and inventing never faded.

By the time he was an adult, Edison had already created several important inventions, including the phonograph (a machine that could record and play sound). But his biggest challenge was yet to come—creating a long-lasting, practical electric light bulb.

At the time, people had tried and failed to create electric light. The idea wasn't new—several inventors had made light bulbs before Edison, but they burned out quickly, were too expensive, or weren't safe for everyday use. Edison believed he could improve the design and make a light bulb that could stay on for hours without burning out.

Edison and his team of inventors at his Menlo Park laboratory in New Jersey began working day and night to find the perfect material for the filament—the tiny wire inside a light bulb that glows when electricity passes through it.

They tested thousands of materials, including paper, cardboard, and even human hair! But nothing lasted long enough. Some filaments burned too fast, while others didn't produce enough light. The team never gave up.

Finally, in 1879, after thousands of failed attempts, Edison and his team found the answer—carbonized bamboo. When placed inside a glass bulb and in a vacuum (with most of the air removed), the filament glowed brightly and lasted for over 1,200 hours. It was a huge breakthrough!

On December 31, 1879, Edison demonstrated his light bulb to the public. He lit up an entire street in Menlo Park, and people were amazed. It was the first time they had ever seen electric light shining brightly in the dark.

But Edison wasn't done yet. He knew that just inventing the light bulb wasn't enough—he had to find a way to bring electricity into homes, streets, and cities. He built the first power station in New York City, allowing people to light their homes with the flip of a switch.

Soon, Edison's invention changed the world. Factories could now stay open at night, homes were brighter and safer, and streets were illuminated, reducing crime and accidents. The invention of the light bulb led to the modern electrical age, powering everything from televisions to computers and smartphones.

Edison's journey wasn't easy. He failed over 1,000 times before finally finding the right design. But he never gave up. He once said, "I have not failed. I've just found 10,000 ways that won't work." His determination and belief in innovation made him one of the most important inventors in history.

Today, light bulbs are everywhere. We don't even think about them when we turn on a lamp or walk under streetlights. But it all started with one man's dream, thousands of experiments, and an unshakable belief in the power of invention.

Because of Thomas Edison's determination, the world went from darkness to light—and life has never been the same since.

The Accidental Invention of the Microwave

Some of the world's greatest inventions were made by accident, and the microwave oven is one of them! Believe it or not, no one set out to create a machine that could heat food in seconds. Instead, it all started with a chocolate bar melting in a man's pocket.

The year was 1945, and a man named Percy Spencer was working in a lab at Raytheon, a company that built radar equipment during World War II. Spencer was an engineer and inventor, always curious about how things worked. On this particular day, he was experimenting with a new type of device called a magnetron—a machine that produced microwaves to help improve radar signals.

While standing close to the magnetron, Spencer felt something unusual. The chocolate bar in his pocket had melted! At first, he didn't think much of it, but then he realized something strange was happening—the microwaves coming from the magnetron had somehow heated the chocolate.

Intrigued, he decided to try something else. He placed a bag of popcorn kernels near the magnetron. To his surprise, the kernels popped into fluffy white popcorn right in front of his eyes! This was the first time anyone had ever cooked food using microwaves.

Excited by his discovery, Spencer decided to experiment further. Next, he put an egg near the magnetron. Before he knew it, the egg exploded all over the lab! That's when he realized that microwaves could heat food quickly and powerfully.

Up until that moment, cooking food always required fire, heat, or boiling water. But Spencer had stumbled upon a completely new way of cooking—using invisible microwaves! He immediately began working on a machine that could safely use microwaves to heat food without melting chocolate in people's pockets or making eggs explode.

Spencer and his team built the first microwave oven. However, it was not like the microwaves we have today. The first microwave was as big as a refrigerator and weighed over 750 pounds! It was also very expensive, costing thousands of dollars, so only restaurants and large businesses could afford to buy one.

Over time, engineers worked to make microwaves smaller, cheaper, and easier to use. By the 1970s, microwaves became affordable for regular households, and soon, almost every kitchen had one. People loved how fast they could heat up leftovers, cook meals, and make popcorn in minutes!

The microwave changed the way people cooked forever. Instead of spending hours cooking on a stove, people could now prepare meals in just a few minutes. Today, microwaves are used in homes, restaurants, offices, and even in space! Astronauts on the International Space Station use microwaves to heat their food while orbiting Earth.

Percy Spencer's discovery was a perfect example of how curiosity and experimentation can lead to incredible inventions. He never planned to invent the microwave—he was simply paying attention to something unusual and decided to explore it further.

Now, every time you heat up a meal in the microwave, remember that it all started because of a melted chocolate bar—and the curiosity of a man who didn't ignore it!

The Birth of the Internet

Imagine a world without the internet—no YouTube, no video games with friends online, no social media, no instant messaging, and no Googling answers to homework. It's hard to believe, but just a few decades ago, the internet didn't exist. Today, we use it for everything—talking to friends, watching videos, shopping, working, learning, and even controlling smart homes. But how did this incredible invention come to be?

The internet wasn't created overnight by one person. It was built over many years by scientists, researchers, and engineers who were trying to solve a problem—how to connect computers so they could talk to each other.

The story of the internet begins in the 1960s, during the Cold War, when the United States feared that enemy attacks could destroy important communication systems. The government wanted a way for computers to send messages even if part of the system was damaged. To solve this, the U.S. Department of Defense created a project called ARPANET (Advanced Research Projects Agency Network (ARPANET)).

In 1969, scientists successfully connected four computers at different universities across the United States. It wasn't fast, and it wasn't user-friendly, but it was the first version of what would become the internet.

The first-ever message sent over ARPANET was meant to say "LOGIN," but the system crashed after the second letter, and the first message in internet history was simply "LO"! Even though it was a small start, it was the beginning of something huge.

Through the 1970s and 1980s, more computers were connected, and scientists improved the way information traveled. Two researchers, Vinton Cerf and Robert Kahn, developed TCP/IP, a set of rules that allowed computers to send and receive data reliably. This system still powers the internet today.

But at that time, the internet was still only used by scientists, researchers, and the military. Regular people had no way to access it. That all changed in 1989, when a British scientist named Tim Berners-Lee invented something that would revolutionize the world—the World Wide Web.

The World Wide Web made the internet easier to use, allowing people to create websites, link information, and access pages with a simple click. In 1991, Berners-Lee launched the first-ever website, and soon, the internet began to spread beyond universities and laboratories.

By the mid-1990s, businesses started building websites, and search engines like Yahoo and Google appeared. Email became a popular way to communicate, and chatrooms allowed people to talk to each other instantly. More and more homes got dial-up internet, which made strange beeping and screeching sounds every time someone connected.

The 2000s brought Wi-Fi, high-speed connections, and social media, changing how people communicated forever. Websites like Facebook, YouTube, and Twitter allowed people to share videos, chat with friends, and stay connected across the globe.

Today, the internet is everywhere—in our phones, cars, schools, and even household appliances. People can video call from opposite sides of the planet, doctors can perform remote surgeries, and self-driving cars use the internet to navigate roads. The internet has even reached outer space, allowing astronauts on the International Space Station to stay connected with Earth.

But the internet is still evolving. Scientists are working on faster networks, quantum internet, and artificial intelligence that could transform the way we interact online.

The internet is one of the most important inventions in history, connecting people in ways that were once only imaginable in science fiction. And to think—it all started with a few computers in a lab and a failed message that said "LO."

So the next time you send a message, watch a video, or play a game online, remember—you're using a technology that changed the world, and its story is still being written!

The Incredible Story of Braille

Louis Braille was born in 1809 in a small town in France. Like any other child, he was curious and playful, always eager to explore the world around him. His father was a leatherworker, and young Louis often watched him craft fine goods in his shop. One day, when Louis was just three years old, he found one of his father's sharp tools, an awl, and began to imitate his father's work. But in an instant, the tool slipped and pierced his eye. The injury quickly became infected, and soon, the infection spread to his other eye. By the time he was five years old, Louis Braille was completely blind.

Despite this tragedy, Louis was determined to learn and succeed. His parents encouraged him, helping him develop a sharp memory and a strong sense of touch to navigate the world. He was a bright and hardworking student, but he soon realized how difficult it was for blind people to read. The few books available for the blind were large and heavy, with raised letters carved into thick paper or wooden boards. These books were slow to read and incredibly expensive, making education difficult for blind students.

At the age of ten, Louis earned a scholarship to attend the Royal Institute for Blind Youth in Paris. It was one of the first schools for blind students, and while he was excited to learn, he struggled with the lack of accessible reading materials. He longed for a better way to read, a system that would allow blind people to experience books just as sighted people did.

In 1821, when Louis was twelve years old, a French soldier named Charles Barbier visited his school. Barbier had developed a special writing system called "night writing," which used raised dots and dashes to allow soldiers to send secret messages in the dark without using light. The system was complicated, but it gave Louis an idea. If he could simplify the concept, he could create a writing method specifically for blind people.

For three years, Louis worked tirelessly, testing different ideas and improving Barbier's system. He discovered that using only dots, rather than dashes, made it easier to read with fingertips. He eventually reduced the system to just six raised dots, arranged in different patterns to represent letters and numbers. By the time he was fifteen years old, he had invented what is now known as Braille—a revolutionary system that would allow blind people to read and write efficiently.

Excited about his discovery, Louis shared his invention with his teachers. However, many people dismissed it, believing that blind people did not need books or that learning Braille would be too complicated. But Louis refused to give up. He spent years teaching his classmates how to use the system, and soon, they realized that Braille was far superior to any other reading method available for the blind. Slowly, more and more students began using it, proving that it was practical and effective.

Even though Braille's invention was brilliant, it was not widely accepted during his lifetime. Schools and institutions resisted change, and Louis never saw his system gain the recognition it deserved. He continued to teach and advocate for his method, but in 1852, at just 43 years old, he passed away without ever knowing that his work would change the world.

A few years after his death, educators and schools for the blind finally recognized the incredible potential of Braille. His system spread across Europe and the United States, becoming the official reading and writing method for blind people worldwide. Today, Braille is used in hundreds of languages and appears on books, signs, elevators, ATMs, and even medicine bottles.

Louis Braille's story is one of perseverance, determination, and innovation. He was just a teenager when he invented something that would give millions of people the gift of literacy and independence. His life proves that one person, no matter how young, can make a difference with creativity and a desire to help others.

The First Artificial Heart

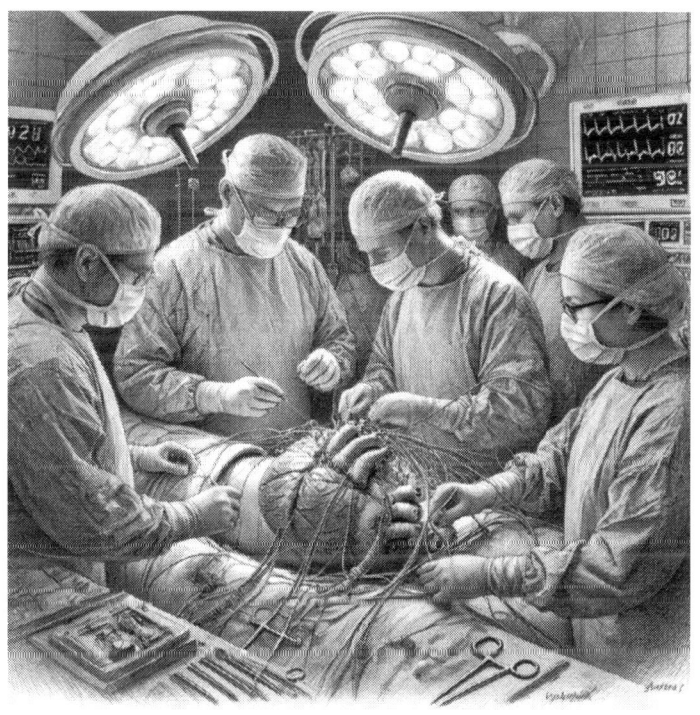

For centuries, doctors and scientists dreamed of finding a way to replace the human heart. The heart is one of the most important organs in the body, pumping blood and oxygen to keep people alive. But when a person's heart becomes too weak or damaged, even the best medicine and surgeries cannot always save them. This led to one of the most groundbreaking inventions in medical history—the first artificial heart.

The idea of replacing a failing heart with a machine seemed like something from a science fiction story. The human heart is an incredibly complex organ, beating over 100,000 times a day and adjusting its speed based on the body's needs. Creating a device that could do the same job was an enormous challenge. But in the 20th century, medical scientists made huge leaps in technology, and the dream of an artificial heart started to become a reality.

In the 1950s and 60s, doctors experimented with heart-lung machines that could temporarily take over the heart's job during surgery. These machines kept patients alive while doctors operated, but they were too large and complex to be used as a permanent heart replacement. However, one doctor, Dr. Paul Winchell, an inventor and ventriloquist, designed an early version of an artificial heart in the 1960s. His design laid the foundation for future breakthroughs.

The real breakthrough came in the 1980s when a heart surgeon named Dr. Barney Clark became the first person in history to receive a permanent artificial heart. Dr. Clark was gravely ill, and his heart was failing. He agreed to undergo an experimental surgery, knowing that it could be his only chance to survive.

On December 2, 1982, Dr. Barney Clark's diseased heart was removed, and in its place, doctors implanted a mechanical heart called the Jarvik-7. This artificial heart was made of plastic and metal, powered by an external machine that had to stay connected to the patient at all times. Unlike a natural heart, it did not beat—it pumped blood using air pressure.

When Dr. Clark woke up after the surgery, the world watched in amazement. He was the first human to live with a completely artificial heart. However, the technology was still in its early stages, and living with the Jarvik-7 was not easy. Dr. Clark remained in the hospital, connected to machines that kept his artificial heart working. He survived for 112 days before passing away due to complications. Though his time with the artificial heart was short, his surgery proved that a mechanical heart could keep a person alive.

In the years that followed, scientists and doctors worked to improve artificial hearts. The goal was to create smaller, more efficient devices that could allow people to live longer and with more freedom.

Today, artificial hearts have advanced significantly. Devices like the SynCardia Total Artificial Heart are used to keep patients alive while they wait for a heart transplant. Some artificial hearts are fully implantable, meaning patients can go home and live their lives with a battery-powered heart instead of being confined to a hospital.

The future of artificial hearts is even more exciting. Scientists are working on biomechanical hearts, which combine artificial materials with living tissue, and 3D-printed hearts, made from human cells. These innovations could one day eliminate the need for heart transplants, saving millions of lives.

The invention of the first artificial heart was a major turning point in medical history. Though it began as an experiment, it opened the door to life-saving technology that continues to improve. Thanks to the courage of pioneers like Dr. Barney Clark, and the dedication of scientists and doctors, artificial hearts have given countless people a second chance at life. The journey is far from over, and one day, artificial hearts may become as common as pacemakers or prosthetic limbs, allowing people with heart disease to live long, healthy lives.

Section 6: Record-Breaking Feats and Extraordinary Human Achievements

The Tallest Building in the World

For centuries, humans have dreamed of building taller and taller structures, pushing the limits of engineering and architecture. From the Great Pyramids of Egypt to the towering skyscrapers of today, people have always looked toward the sky for inspiration. But no building in history has ever reached as high as the Burj Khalifa, the tallest building in the world. Standing in Dubai, United Arab Emirates, this incredible skyscraper is a symbol of innovation, ambition, and modern engineering.

The Burj Khalifa is 828 meters (2,717 feet) tall, making it almost twice as tall as the Empire State Building in New York. It has 163 floors, and from the very top, visitors can see for miles in every direction. The building is so tall that someone standing at the top floor can see the sunset twice—once from the ground and again when they reach the top.

Before the Burj Khalifa, many buildings held the title of world's tallest. The Eiffel Tower in Paris was once the tallest structure in the world in the late 1800s. Later, skyscrapers like the Chrysler Building and the Empire State Building in New York took over the record. In 2004, the Taipei 101 in Taiwan became the world's tallest building at 508 meters (1,667 feet). But Dubai had a much bigger vision—to build something the world had never seen before.

The construction of the Burj Khalifa began in 2004, and it took six years to complete. Thousands of engineers, architects, and workers from all over the world came together to design and build the skyscraper. It was a massive challenge because a building this tall had never been built before.

One of the biggest challenges was keeping the building stable against strong winds. Since Dubai is located in a desert, windstorms and sandstorms can be extremely powerful. To solve this, engineers designed the Burj Khalifa with a special Y-shaped structure that helps it resist strong winds. The building is also made of reinforced concrete and steel, making it strong enough to withstand earthquakes and extreme weather.

Another major challenge was getting water and electricity to such a tall building. The Burj Khalifa has one of the most advanced water supply systems in the world, pumping water up hundreds of meters so that people on the highest floors can have running water. It also has an advanced air conditioning system that cools the air using water collected from the humid desert atmosphere.

The Burj Khalifa officially opened on January 4, 2010, and quickly became one of the most famous landmarks in the world. It houses luxury apartments, offices, hotels, restaurants, and even a swimming pool on the 76th floor.

The highest observation deck in the world, located on the 148th floor, allows visitors to look down at the clouds from above. At night, the building lights up with dazzling LED displays, and during special events, it becomes a giant screen for fireworks and laser shows.

One of the most interesting facts about the Burj Khalifa is that it can be seen from nearly 95 kilometers (60 miles) away. It is so tall that, on the higher floors, time moves slightly faster due to the effects of gravity—something predicted by Einstein's Theory of Relativity!

Even though the Burj Khalifa is the tallest building in the world today, engineers are already working on building even taller skyscrapers. In Saudi Arabia, the Jeddah Tower, expected to be over 1,000 meters (3,280 feet) tall, is under construction and may soon take the title of world's tallest building.

The Burj Khalifa is more than just a skyscraper—it is a symbol of human achievement and determination. It proves that with vision, innovation, and teamwork, there are no limits to what we can build. Whether or not another building surpasses it in the future, the Burj Khalifa will always hold a special place in history as the tower that reached for the sky and changed the world of architecture forever.

The First Journey to the Top

For centuries, Mount Everest stood as an unconquered giant, the highest peak on Earth, towering 8,849 meters (29,032 feet) above sea level. Located on the border between Nepal and Tibet, Everest had long been a place of awe and danger, with its freezing temperatures, deadly avalanches, and dangerously thin air. Many brave climbers had attempted to reach the summit, but for years, the mountain defeated them all. Then, in 1953, two courageous men finally achieved what no one had done before—they became the first humans to stand at the top of the world.

The journey to conquer Everest had begun many years earlier. In the 1920s and 1930s, several expeditions tried and failed. Some climbers disappeared in the snow, never to be seen again. Others turned back just short of the summit, defeated by exhaustion, frostbite, or lack of oxygen. Many believed Everest was simply too dangerous to climb. But that didn't stop adventurers from trying.

In 1953, the British Everest Expedition set out with a new plan. The team included some of the best climbers in the world, but two names would become legendary— Edmund Hillary, a beekeeper and mountaineer from New Zealand, and Tenzing Norgay, a highly skilled Sherpa climber from Nepal. The Sherpas, native to the Himalayas, were known for their incredible strength and ability to survive at high altitudes.

The expedition began in March 1953, with the team slowly making its way through the treacherous ice fields and steep cliffs. The climbers had to carry heavy loads of supplies, battling against freezing winds, blizzards, and deadly crevasses—deep cracks in the ice that could swallow a person whole. They also had to climb through the Khumbu Icefall, one of the most dangerous sections of the mountain, where massive ice towers could collapse at any moment.

As they climbed higher, the air became dangerously thin. At such altitudes, oxygen levels are so low that climbers suffer from altitude sickness, making them dizzy, weak, and confused. To survive, Hillary and Tenzing used oxygen tanks, a relatively new idea at the time.

After weeks of slow, painful progress, the team set up their final camp at 8,500 meters (27,900 feet). From here, only two climbers could make the final push to the top. The first team attempted the summit but had to turn back due to oxygen problems. Then, on May 28, 1953, Edmund Hillary and Tenzing Norgay were given their chance.

The next morning, at 4:00 AM, they began their final climb. Every step was a battle against the freezing cold and exhaustion. The snow was deep and unstable, and every movement was painfully slow. Then, they reached a massive, steep rock face, now known as the Hillary Step. Climbing it was extremely dangerous, but Hillary found a narrow way up, pulling himself over the edge. Finally, at 11:30 AM on May 29, 1953, after hours of struggle, they reached the summit. They stood on the highest point on Earth, looking down at the world below. For the first time in history, humans had conquered Mount Everest.

Tenzing planted the flags of Nepal, India, and Britain, while Hillary took photographs. The two climbers shook hands, but Tenzing later recalled that in his excitement, he hugged Hillary instead. They spent only 15 minutes at the top, knowing they had to descend quickly before bad weather set in. When they returned to camp, the rest of the team celebrated their incredible achievement. News of their success spread quickly, and by the time they reached Kathmandu, they were greeted as heroes. Edmund Hillary was knighted by Queen Elizabeth II, becoming Sir Edmund Hillary, and Tenzing Norgay became a national hero in Nepal.

Their achievement proved that even the most impossible dreams can come true with courage, determination, and teamwork. Today, thousands of climbers attempt to reach Everest's peak each year, following in the footsteps of the two men who first stood at the top of the world.

The Longest Time Living Underwater

For most people, staying underwater for a few minutes while swimming is a challenge. But what if someone lived underwater for months? It might sound like something from a science fiction movie, but in 2023, a man named Dr. Joseph Dituri broke a world record by living underwater for 100 days straight. His incredible journey was not just about setting a record—it was an experiment to learn how the human body adapts to long-term underwater living, which could help scientists prepare for deep-sea exploration and space travel.

Dr. Joseph Dituri, also known as "Dr. Deep Sea," is a former U.S. Navy officer and professor of biomedical engineering. He has always been fascinated by the ocean and the effects of extreme environments on the human body. His record-breaking mission began on March 1, 2023, when he entered the Jules' Undersea Lodge, an underwater habitat located 30 feet (9 meters) beneath the ocean's surface in Key Largo, Florida.

The lodge is a small, pressurized research station, originally designed for marine scientists to study underwater life. It is about 100 square feet in size—smaller than a typical bedroom—so living there for over three months was no easy task. Unlike a submarine, which moves through the water, Jules' Undersea Lodge is a fixed habitat, meaning Dituri could not surface unless he ended the experiment.

Life underwater was very different from life on land. There was no sunlight, and Dituri had to rely on artificial lights to maintain his daily routine. He had access to oxygen, water, and food, but everything had to be delivered by divers. His meals included high-protein foods like eggs, fish, and peanut butter, but he had to carefully manage his supplies to ensure they lasted.

One of the biggest challenges of living underwater for so long was dealing with high pressure. The deeper a person goes into the ocean, the more pressure the water exerts on the body. At 30 feet below the surface, the pressure is about twice as high as it is on land. Scientists were curious to see how this would affect Dituri's health, brain function, and aging process.

Throughout the experiment, Dituri continued his work as a professor, teaching online classes from inside his underwater home. He also exercised daily, doing push-ups and resistance training to keep his muscles strong in the cramped space. Since he couldn't go outside for a walk, staying active was crucial to staying healthy.

One of the most interesting parts of the experiment was studying how living underwater affected Dituri's body. Scientists regularly checked his blood pressure, sleep patterns, and mental health to see how he was adapting. Surprisingly, the results were better than expected—

Dituri reported feeling stronger and healthier, and researchers even noticed a slowing of his biological aging process. His body seemed to be aging more slowly than it would have on land, leading scientists to wonder if pressurized environments could help people live longer.

Another important goal of the experiment was to understand how humans could survive in isolated, extreme environments. This research is not only useful for underwater exploration but also for space missions. If humans ever live on Mars or the Moon, they will need to stay in small, pressurized habitats for long periods, just like Dituri did underwater.

After 100 days, on June 9, 2023, Dituri finally resurfaced, setting a new world record for the longest time living underwater without depressurization. As he emerged from the water, he was greeted by a team of scientists, journalists, and supporters who had followed his journey. Despite spending over three months beneath the ocean, he felt strong and full of energy, proving that humans are capable of adapting to incredible challenges.

Dr. Dituri's underwater mission was more than just a record-breaking stunt—it was a scientific breakthrough. His experiment provided valuable insights into human endurance, health, and future space travel, showing that the deep sea and outer space have more in common than we ever imagined. His adventure inspires scientists, astronauts, and explorers to keep pushing the limits of what humans can achieve. Who knows? One day, we may see people living not just underwater—but on other planets as well.

Felix Baumgartner's Jump from Space

On October 14, 2012, millions of people around the world held their breath as they watched a man step out of a tiny capsule, floating high above Earth's atmosphere. Felix Baumgartner, an Austrian skydiver and daredevil, was about to do something that had never been done before—jump from the edge of space, breaking multiple world records in the process. His incredible leap was not just a thrilling stunt but also a scientific experiment, helping researchers understand how humans could survive in extreme conditions.

Felix Baumgartner was no ordinary skydiver. He had spent years performing dangerous base jumps, leaping from skyscrapers, bridges, and cliffs. But this challenge was unlike anything he had ever attempted. He partnered with Red Bull Stratos, a mission designed to push the limits of human endurance and test the effects of high-altitude jumps on the human body. Scientists hoped the mission would provide valuable information for future space travel and emergency escape systems.

The plan was simple but extremely risky. Felix would ride a giant helium balloon into the stratosphere, a layer of Earth's atmosphere far higher than where airplanes fly. Once he reached 39 kilometers (24 miles) above Earth, he would jump—falling faster than the speed of sound before parachuting safely to the ground.

The journey began early in the morning in Roswell, New Mexico, where Felix climbed into a pressurized spacesuit, specially designed to protect him from freezing temperatures and lack of oxygen at high altitudes. He then squeezed into a tiny capsule, which was attached to the helium balloon. As the balloon slowly ascended, he became the highest human ever to ascend without an aircraft.

For more than two hours, Felix floated higher and higher, reaching the edge of space. Below him, Earth stretched out in a breathtaking view—a blue planet surrounded by the blackness of space. But while the view was beautiful, the danger was very real. If his suit failed, his blood could boil due to the low pressure, or he could lose consciousness from lack of oxygen.

Finally, at 39,045 meters (128,100 feet)—three times higher than commercial airplanes fly—Felix opened the capsule door. He stood at the edge, looked down at Earth, and took a deep breath. Then, he jumped. The moment Felix leaped from the capsule, he began to fall faster than any human had ever fallen. Within seconds, he broke the sound barrier, meaning he was traveling faster than the speed of sound—1,357 km/h (843 mph). No human had ever done this without a vehicle before. As he plummeted through the sky, Felix spun out of control, tumbling violently in the thin air. If he didn't regain control, he could have lost consciousness, which would have been deadly. But after several terrifying seconds, he managed to stabilize himself, focusing on keeping his body positioned correctly. After falling for 4 minutes and 20 seconds, he deployed his parachute, slowing his descent. The crowd watching on the ground erupted in cheers as they saw his parachute open. Moments later, Felix landed safely in the New Mexico desert, where his team rushed to greet him. He had survived one of the most extreme jumps in history.

Felix Baumgartner's jump from space broke several world records:

• He became the first human to break the sound barrier without an aircraft.

• He set the record for the highest freefall jump.

• He achieved the fastest speed ever reached in freefall.

More importantly, his jump provided valuable data for scientists and astronauts. The mission helped researchers develop better spacesuits and safety measures for high-altitude pilots and future space travelers. Felix Baumgartner's daring leap proved that humans are capable of incredible feats of bravery and innovation. His record-breaking jump remains one of the most thrilling achievements in the history of space exploration and skydiving.

The Fastest Human on Earth

In the world of sports, few athletes have ever dominated their field the way Usain Bolt did. Known as the fastest human on Earth, he became a legend in track and field, shattering world records and winning Olympic gold medals with ease. But what made Usain Bolt truly special wasn't just his speed—it was his charisma, confidence, and love for the sport, which made him one of the most popular and inspiring athletes of all time.

Usain Bolt was born on August 21, 1986, in Sherwood Content, Jamaica, a small rural town where he grew up playing cricket and soccer. As a child, he loved sports but didn't think much about running at first. However, his coaches noticed something special—he was incredibly fast. Even as a teenager, he could outrun almost anyone. At the age of 15, Bolt won the World Junior Championships, becoming the youngest athlete ever to win a gold medal in the 200-meter sprint. His talent was undeniable, but his journey to greatness was just beginning.

Standing at 6 feet 5 inches tall, Bolt was unlike most sprinters. Typically, shorter athletes were considered better suited for sprinting because they could accelerate faster. But Bolt's long legs and powerful stride gave him a unique advantage. Once he reached top speed, no one could catch him.

Despite his natural talent, Bolt faced setbacks and injuries early in his career. Many doubted whether he could compete at the highest level, but he remained determined. His big breakthrough came in 2008, at the Beijing Olympics, where he stunned the world.

In the 100-meter final, Bolt not only won the race but did something never seen before. With 20 meters still to go, he looked around, spread his arms, and celebrated before even crossing the finish line. The crowd went wild. He finished in 9.69 seconds, setting a new world record and becoming the Olympic champion. Just days later, he did it again, breaking the 200-meter world record, becoming the first man in history to set world records in both sprints at the same Olympics.

After his historic performance in Beijing, Bolt became a global superstar. His signature "Lightning Bolt" pose—where he pointed to the sky after each victory—became famous worldwide. Fans loved his fun personality and playful attitude, which made him stand out from other serious athletes. But behind the smiles, he trained harder than ever.

In 2009, at the World Championships in Berlin, Bolt did the impossible. He broke his own world record in the 100 meters, running an astonishing 9.58 seconds—a time that no one has beaten to this day. He also shattered the 200-

meter world record, finishing in 19.19 seconds. These times made him the fastest person to ever run on Earth.

Over the next decade, Bolt continued to dominate sprinting. He won eight Olympic gold medals and became an 11-time world champion. No sprinter in history had ever achieved so much. He remained unbeatable in major races, proving time and time again that he was the greatest sprinter of all time.

Even though he was the fastest man on Earth, Bolt always remembered to have fun. He danced before races, joked with reporters, and entertained fans with his outgoing personality. His love for competition and ability to perform under pressure made him a role model for athletes everywhere.

In 2017, after nearly a decade of dominance, Bolt retired from professional sprinting. His impact on the sport, however, remains legendary. Today, young athletes still look up to him, and his world records remain untouched.

Usain Bolt's story is one of talent, hard work, and confidence. He didn't just run fast—he made sprinting exciting and inspired millions to chase their dreams. Whether or not anyone ever breaks his records, Bolt will always be remembered as the greatest sprinter in history and the fastest man to ever live.

Conclusion

The world is filled with amazing true stories, and the ones in this book are just the beginning. From record-breaking athletes to mysterious disappearances, from scientific discoveries to incredible adventures, each story shows just how extraordinary our world can be. These aren't just tales from history or science they are stories of bravery, curiosity, and determination.

Think about Felix Baumgartner, who jumped from space, or Usain Bolt, who became the fastest human on Earth. Their achievements show that with courage and hard work, people can push the limits of what seems possible. Then, there's Louis Braille, who didn't let blindness stop him from creating a new way to read, changing the lives of millions. Or Thomas Edison, who failed thousands of times before inventing the light bulb. These stories remind us that success often comes from never giving up, no matter how difficult the journey.

The mysteries in this book—like the Bermuda Triangle, the Mary Celeste, and the Green Children of Woolpit—remind us that the world is full of unanswered questions. Scientists and explorers are still trying to solve these puzzles, proving that there is always something new to discover. Who knows? Maybe one day, someone reading this book will find the answers to these unsolved mysteries!

Nature, too, has its own incredible stories. Monarch butterflies travel thousands of miles in their great migration, octopuses escape from their tanks with their brilliant minds, and black holes, once thought to be invisible, were finally photographed for the first time. The world is full of wonders, and as technology improves, we will continue to unlock the secrets of our universe.

But the most exciting part? There are still so many stories yet to be written. Every day, people around the world are breaking records, solving mysteries, and inventing new things. Maybe the next great discovery will come from someone just like you! If you love to ask questions, explore new ideas, or challenge yourself, you could be the next scientist, athlete, adventurer, or inventor whose story will inspire the world.

The stories in this book are proof that anything is possible. Whether it's climbing the tallest mountain, jumping from space, creating a world-changing invention, or running faster than anyone in history, human potential is limitless. The world is waiting for new explorers, dreamers, and problem-solvers to step up and make their mark.

So, what will your story be? Will you discover something new, break a record, or solve a great mystery? The future is full of possibilities, and the most exciting part is that you get to decide what happens next. Keep exploring, keep asking questions, and never stop believing that you can do something amazing too!

Printed in Great Britain
by Amazon